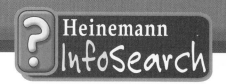

Living in a
Desert

Heinemann Library
Chicago, Illinois

Carol Baldwin

Customer Service 888-454-2279

Visit our website at www.heinemannlibrary.com

Designed by Kimberly Saar, Heinemann Library
Illustrations and maps by John Fleck
Photo research by Bill Broyles
Printed and bound in the United States by Lake Book Manufacturing, Inc.

07 06 05 04 03
10 9 8 7 6 5 4 3 2 1

Library of Congress Cataloging-in-Publication Data
Baldwin, Carol, 1943-
  Living in a desert / Carol Baldwin.
      v. cm. -- (Living habitats)
Includes index..
Contents: What makes land a desert? -- Why are deserts important? -- How can plants grow in deserts? -- How do animals live in a desert? -- What's for dinner in the desert? -- How do desert animals get food? -- How do people live in deserts? -- How have people affected deserts?
  ISBN 1-40340-840-8 (lib. bdg. : hardcover)
  1. Desert ecology--Juvenile literature. [1. Desert ecology. 2. Deserts. 3. Ecology.] I. Title.
  QH541.5.D4 B365 2003
  577.54--dc21
                              2002011353

Acknowledgments
The author and publishers are grateful to the following for permission to reproduce copyright material:
p. 4 Stefano Nicolini/Animals Animals; p. 5 Medford Taylor/National Geographic; p. 6 Stuart Franklin/Magnum Photos; p. 7 Francois Gohier/Photo Researchers, Inc.; p. 8 Clem Haagner/Photo Researchers, Inc.; p. 9 Joyce & Frank Burek/Animals Animals; pp. 10, 16 Fletcher & Baylis/Photo Researchers, Inc.; p. 11 Konrad Wothe/Minden Pictures; p. 11 (inset) Gary Braasch/Corbis; p. 12 Peter Chadwick/Science Photo Library; p. 13 A. Bannister/OSF/ Animals Animals; p. 14 Steve Kaufman/Corbis; p. 15 Alain Dragesco-Joffe/Animals Animals; p. 17 Stuart Westmorland/Photo Researchers, Inc.; p. 18 Charlie Ott/Photo Researchers, Inc.; p. 20 Richard T. Nowitz/Corbis; p. 21 George Holton/Photo Researchers, Inc.; p. 22 Yann Arthus-Bertrand/Corbis; p. 23 Walt Anderson/Visuals Unlimited; p. 24 Mark Boulton/Photo Researchers, Inc.; p. 25 R. & E. Thane/Animals Animals; p. 26 Dinodia; p. 27 Ray Ellis/Photo Researchers, Inc.

Cover photograph: Francois Gohier/Photo Researchers, Inc.

Some words are shown in bold, **like this**. You can find out what they mean by looking in the glossary.

Contents

What Makes Land a Desert?

The Atacama Desert in Chile is the world's driest desert. Once, no rain fell there for over 40 years.

The sun blazes down on sand as far as the eye can see. There is no escape from the heat. This is a desert. A cold wind blasts over dry, stony ground. This, too, is a desert. How can both these places be deserts?

Deserts are always dry

A desert is a place that is very dry. Few clouds form over deserts. The sun is almost always shining. Even the wettest deserts get less than 10 inches (25 centimeters) of rain in a year. Some parts of a desert might get rain, while other parts don't. Rain that does fall often **evaporates** before it can reach the ground. Sometimes a desert goes for years without any rain.

Temperature doesn't matter

Some deserts are hot. The Mojave Desert in the southwestern United States is a hot desert. But even in a hot desert, you would feel cold at night. Temperatures in the Mojave can reach 119 °F (48 °C) or drop to 8 °F (−13 °C). Some deserts are cold, and snow may fall. The Gobi Desert in Asia is a cold desert.

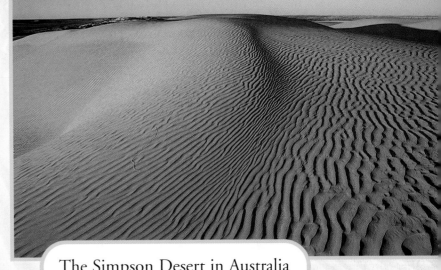

The Simpson Desert in Australia has the longest sand dunes in the world. Notice how they form in straight rows.

Deserts don't have to be sandy

Many deserts are not covered with sand. Wind **erodes** desert rocks to form sand. But wind also carries sand away in some areas. This exposes rocks and stones on the desert surface. Sandy deserts have large sand **dunes.** The Arabian Desert has some of the largest areas of sand dunes in the world. Large parts of the Mojave Desert have a stony surface. Other parts have sandy soil.

❓ Did you know?

Part of the Arabian Desert is known as the Empty Quarter. It's a huge area of sand that's almost as big as the state of Texas.

Why Are Deserts Important?

People used to think of deserts as wastelands. Deserts seem to have few plants and animals. Few people seem to live in deserts. But this isn't really true.

Oil has brought great wealth to some desert nations such as Saudi Arabia and Kuwait.

Deserts have resources people use

About a billion people live in Earth's deserts. Most of these people live in and around **oases.** Oases form where underground water comes to the desert's surface. People can raise crops and animals here.

Many deserts have other things people use. The Sahara and Arabian Deserts have large amounts of oil and natural gas. The Atacama Desert has **minerals** that are used to make fertilizers for farms. The Gobi Desert is rich in copper, gold, and oil. Australia's deserts have iron, gold, and other minerals. Diamonds are found in the deserts of southern Africa.

? Did you know?

Gold has been mined from Australian deserts for about 150 years.

The first fossil eggs of a meat-eating dinosaur were found in the Gobi in 1993.

Deserts are homes to living things

Many desert plants and animals are found nowhere else on Earth. More plants and animals live in deserts than you might think. The Sahara has more than a thousand different kinds of plants. The Sonoran Desert, in Arizona, California, and Mexico, has more animals than any other desert in the world.

Deserts preserve fossils

Because deserts are dry, they are good places for **fossils** to be preserved. Some of the best fossils of animals have been found in deserts.

About 80 million years ago, many animals were gathered at an oasis in the Gobi Desert. Huge sandstorms killed and buried the animals. They turned into fossils. Many different kinds of dinosaur fossils have been found in the Gobi. Fossil dinosaur eggs have also been found. Other important fossils have been found in the Sahara.

How Do Plants Live in Deserts?

3

Desert plants have special **adaptations.** These are features that allow them to live in places that are very dry. Because of this, desert plants often look very different than plants found in other places. What are these special features?

Plants keep water

Some desert plants have waxy coatings. These keep them from losing water their roots take in. Aloe plants live in the Kalahari and Namib Deserts in Africa. Their waxy coating acts like a plastic wrapper that keeps water inside.

Plant leaves have little holes, called **stomata,** on their bottom sides. These little holes let gases go into and out of the plants.

Big sagebrush has big leaves only in the spring. They fall off in the summer. The leaves that it grows year-round are smaller. These have few stomata. Small leaves help keep water inside the plant from **evaporating.**

Aloe plants, like others with waxy coatings, are called **succulents.**

Plants store water

Some plants store water in their stems or leaves. The kokerboom tree grows in the deserts of southwestern Africa. It stores water in its trunk.

Barrel cactuses have a pleated shape like an accordion. When it rains, the cactus takes water from the ground. Its pleats spread open and it grows larger. The cactus uses the stored water during dry times. As it uses water, it shrinks and the pleats close up.

Some cactuses and other desert plants have thorns. Thorns protect them from **grazing** animals. This is a saguaro cactus.

Saguaro cactuses are the tallest cactuses. They can grow to more than 50 feet (17 meters) tall. A saguaro's large net of roots grows far out from the trunk. The roots collect water after it rains. The stored water keeps the saguaro alive until the next rain. A large saguaro can store tons of water in its pleated trunk.

? **Did you know?**

Africa's baobab tree can store up to 30,000 gallons (114,000 liters) of water in its trunk.

Plants grow long roots

Mesquite trees are very common in deserts of the southwestern United States. Mesquite trees have the longest roots of any desert plant. Their roots are able to draw water from more than 100 feet (30 meters) under the ground.

Creosote bushes have both deep and shallow roots. When it rains, the shallow roots quickly take up water that falls on the ground. During dry times, the deep roots get water from deep in the ground. Creosote bushes can live for a year without rain. Joshua trees are another kind of plant with long roots. They grow only in the Mojave Desert.

The onion-of-the-desert plant grows in the Namib Desert. It has only two leaves that grow very slowly. Its large, long root reaches deep underground for water. It can store water in this root.

The onion-of-the-desert plant can live for hundreds of years.

The stems of the ocotillo plant can be from 9 to 30 feet (3 to 9 meters) tall. Each stem has spines. Other names for the plant include vine cactus and coach whip.

Plants wait for rain

The ocotillo plant is found in Mexico and the southwestern United States. During most of the year, this plant does not have any leaves. After it rains, the leaves grow quickly. When the soil dries out, the leaves wither and die. The ocotillo plant can grow leaves several times a year, after each rain. If there is no rain, the plant's flowers can still bloom even if there are no leaves.

Grasses grow in some deserts, such as the Gobi. Grasses have long, thin roots that spread over a wide area. During dry times, the parts of the plants above the ground might die. But the roots stay alive. When the rain comes, new grass sprouts from the ground. Grasses are important for holding the thin desert soil in place.

? Did you know?

As much as nine-tenths of the weight of grass plants is in the roots.

4 How Do Animals Live in Deserts?

Like desert plants, desert animals have **adaptations.** These include how the animals live and behave. They also include special body parts that help animals live in the desert.

Some seek shade

Many animals in hot deserts spend the day in the shade. The African ground squirrel lives in the Kalahari Desert. It can make its own shade by lifting its long, fluffy tail and covering its body.

Other animals stay under rocks or in **burrows** under the ground. Gerbils and jerboas live in both hot and cold deserts in Africa and Asia. They dig burrows in the ground. These underground homes protect them from both hot and cold weather.

Toads usually live near water holes in the desert. Some, like the spadefoot toad, dig a deep hole in the ground. They come out only when it rains.

The African ground squirrel eats leaves, seeds, nuts, fruits, and sometimes reptiles, insects, and birds' eggs.

Different kinds of scorpions live in deserts all over the world.

Some avoid the day

Some animals are active only in late evening and early morning. At these times, the desert is not too hot and not too cold. Khurs are relatives of burros and donkeys. They live in the deserts of Asia. Small groups travel great distances in the morning and evening looking for food.

Many desert animals are **nocturnal.** They are active only at night. The desert seems to come alive after dark. That's when most animals come out of their burrows. Elf owls of the North American deserts spend their days in old woodpecker nests inside cactuses. At night, they come out to search for insects. Snakes and scorpions also come out at night to hunt for food.

? Did you know?

People who study scorpions use a special ultraviolet (UV) light. In the dark, scorpions glow when UV light shines on them, making them easy to find.

Dorcas gazelles live in the Sahara.

All animals need water

In all deserts, hot or cold, animals must get water. Arabian camels store fat in their single hump. Their bodies are able to change the fat into water and energy. This helps them go without food or water for several days. When they do reach water again, they can gulp down as much as 30 gallons (114 liters) of water in ten minutes. That's equal to drinking about 480 glasses of water.

The sand grouse nests in the African desert. The male flies as far as 50 miles (80 kilometers) to a water hole. He stands in the water hole while he drinks. His feathers soak up water. Then he flies back to the chicks. They suck the water from his feathers.

Dorcas gazelles get most of their water from plants they eat. Kangaroo rats and African gerbils never drink water. They get all their water from the seeds they eat.

Body adaptations help animals

Fennec foxes live in the hot deserts of northern Africa. They are the world's smallest foxes. Large ears allow heat to escape from a fennec fox's body. This keeps it cool during the day. Thick fur keeps the fox warm during the cold desert nights.

Bactrian camels live in the cold deserts of Asia. Thick, shaggy coats protect them from winter temperatures that reach −20 °F (−29 °C). Summer temperatures can be higher than 100 °F (38 °C). In summer, camels shed their heavy coats. Bactrian camels also have tough feet for crossing the rocky deserts. Camels have two rows of eyelashes. Their ears are lined with hairs. They can also close their lips and nose tightly. These features help protect them from blowing sand or snow.

The light-colored fur of the fennec fox takes in less heat than dark fur would.

5 What's for Dinner in a Desert?

All life, in all **habitats,** begins with plants. Animals eat the plants. Other animals eat the plant-eaters.

Plants

Plants make, or produce, their own food. They are called **producers.** Plants like cactuses, grasses, and acacias are producers that grow in deserts. They make food from carbon dioxide gas in the air and water from their roots. Plants need energy to change the carbon dioxide and water into sugars. The energy comes from sunlight. This process is called **photosynthesis.**

Animals

Animals are called **consumers** because they eat, or consume, food. Some desert animals, such as camels, eat only plants. These animals are called **herbivores.** Other animals, such as fennec foxes, eat both plants and animals. They are called **omnivores.** Still others, such as scorpions and rattlesnakes, eat only animals. They are called **carnivores.**

Acacias are producers that live in hot deserts.

The clean-up crew

Other kinds of consumers feed on dead plants and animals and their waste. They are called **decomposers.** **Bacteria, molds,** and some beetles are decomposers. Without them, dead plants and animals would pile up everywhere.

Dung beetles are nature's "pooper scoopers."

Dung beetles feed on animal droppings, or **dung.** They roll the dung into a ball. Then they dig a hole and lay their eggs on the ball. The buried dung is a food source for the beetle **larvae** when they hatch from eggs.

Decomposers break down **nutrients** stored in dead plants and animals. They put the nutrients back into the soil, air, and water. Then plants use the nutrients to help them grow.

Too few decomposers

In some deserts, it's so dry that few decomposers can survive. Dead animals sometimes dry out before the few decomposers can break down their bodies. The animal bodies become **mummified.**

17

How Do Desert Animals Get Food?

Roadrunners can fly, but usually don't. They run after their food.

Some animals hunt other animals. Other animals **scavenge** or **forage.**

Hunting

Animals that hunt and kill other animals for food are **predators.** Roadrunners are predators. They chase down and eat insects, lizards, and small snakes. Desert night lizards eat plants such as yucca. But they also hunt and eat termites, ants, and beetles. So they are predators. Animals that predators eat are **prey.** Insects are prey of lizards and roadrunners.

Some desert animals are both predators and prey. Sidewinder rattlesnakes eat mice, rats, and lizards. This means they are predators. However, small rattlesnakes are also eaten by roadrunners. So they are also prey.

Foragers

Some animals, such as camels and gazelles, are **foragers.** They move about, sometimes in groups, to search for food. Sometimes they have to travel great distances to find food in the desert.

Scavenging

Vultures are desert **scavengers.** Scavengers are animals that eat the bodies of other animals that are already dead. Vultures soar on huge wings, searching for food. Their strong, hooked beaks can easily cut into the flesh of dead animals.

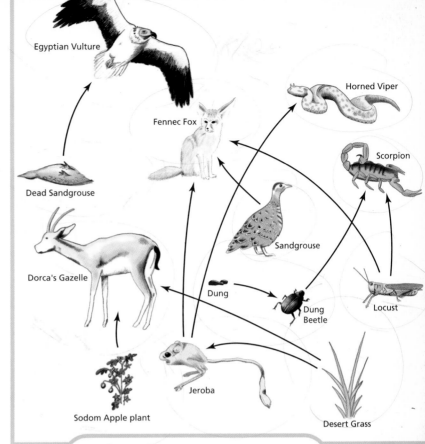

Egyptian Vulture

Dead Sandgrouse

Fennec Fox

Horned Viper

Scorpion

Sandgrouse

Dorca's Gazelle

Dung

Dung Beetle

Locust

Jeroba

Sodom Apple plant

Desert Grass

Planning the menu

The path that shows who eats what is a **food chain.** All living

In a food web, an arrow is drawn from "dinner," or prey, and points to the "diner," or predator.

things are parts of food chains. In the Sahara, locusts eat desert grass. Then, scorpions eat locusts. Another desert food chain includes the seeds of desert grass, jerboas, and snakes called horned vipers. All the food chains that are connected in a **habitat** make up a **food web.**

? Did you know?

Turkey vultures are one of the few kinds of birds that have a good sense of smell. In one experiment, scientists hid food. Even though they were flying high in the sky, the vultures still found it.

7 How Do People Live in Deserts?

It may seem strange to wear a lot of clothes in a hot desert. However, loose robes let air flow underneath. This keeps the person cool.

Most people who have learned to live in deserts are **nomads.** They have to keep moving to find food and water. But in some countries, people have other ways of living in the desert.

Nomads in hot deserts

Bedouins have lived in the deserts of North Africa and Arabia for 2,000 years. They move from one **oasis** to another with herds of animals. Camels carry their tents and other things. Camel's milk and cheese are used as food.

Camel **dung** is burned for cooking and heating. Camel hair is woven into cloth to make clothing and tents.

People need to keep cool during the day and keep warm at night. Long, flowing robes protect bedouins from the hot sun during the day. Robes also help keep them warm during the cold desert nights.

The San people live in the Kalahari Desert of Africa. The people wear little clothing. They travel in small family groups in the coolest parts of the day. They move about once a month to find new food supplies. The men hunt wild animals with bows and arrows. The women gather plants and roots. They store water in empty ostrich eggshells. Their shelters are made from grasses and tree branches.

The tents of nomads in the Gobi Desert are made of wood frames covered with layers of thick **felt** and animal skins.

Nomads in cold deserts

Mongol nomads live in the rocky Gobi Desert. They travel with their sheep, goats, **yaks,** horses, and camels. When their animals have eaten all the grass in one place, they move. They get milk, cheese, butter, and meat from their animals. They make their clothes from wool cloth and sheepskin. Their round tents are called yurts or gers.

Life in deserts is changing

Desert life can be difficult. It's easy to get lost in deserts. Much of the desert looks the same. The few roads through deserts are often covered by blowing sand or dust. Even though **nomads** have traveled in the deserts for thousands of years, many are giving up the desert way of life.

Hospitals, schools, and modern houses in cities make life easier for people who were nomads.

Many bedouins have stopped traveling. Some have settled near water and become farmers. Many others now live and work in the oil fields of the desert. Others have found jobs in towns and cities.

Life is also changing in the Gobi. Instead of camels or horses, some nomads now use trucks to cross the desert. Others have given up moving around. Now they live in villages near larger cities. They work in the cities, but most still live in yurts.

Large cities in deserts

Most deserts don't have large cities. However, the deserts of the United States have some of the fastest-growing cities. Phoenix and Tucson in the Sonoran Desert of Arizona are two of them. Many people have moved to these cities because of the warm, sunny weather. Phoenix has about 310 sunny days each year. The temperature hardly ever goes below freezing. But Phoenix gets less than eight inches (twenty centimeters) of rain each year. So, how do people live in these desert cities?

The cities get water from underground wells and rivers. This water supply has allowed these cities to grow. People use the water to **irrigate** crops and lawns. People also live in air-conditioned homes to avoid the desert heat. They drive air-conditioned cars, and they shop in air-conditioned stores.

Today, eight out of every ten people in Arizona live in deserts.

How Have People Affected Deserts?

Goats can eat all the plants in an area. This takes away food from wild desert animals.

Deserts are growing larger in many places. This process is called **desertification.** It happens because of the way people use the land. In other places, people are working to protect deserts while still using them.

People destroy plants

The land close to the edges of deserts gets a little more rain. Enough plants can grow for animals to **graze** on the grasses and shrubs. If farmers let too many animals graze, the grass and plants may not regrow. Then there are no plants to hold the soil in place. Soil is blown away by wind. The land then becomes desert. The same thing can happen where people cut down too many trees for firewood.

?
Did you know?

In the last 50 years, the Sahara has spread south. It now covers an extra area almost the size of Texas.

People hunt and mine

People have always hunted desert animals. But now people travel faster and farther in trucks. They use guns that desert **nomads** didn't have in the past. It is easier for hunters to find and kill animals. Now, some desert animals are in danger of becoming **extinct.** In the Sahara, several kinds of large antelopes are almost extinct.

The Copper Queen mine in Bisbee, Arizona, was open from 1877 to 1975.

People also damage deserts by mining. Mining for certain **minerals** uses huge amounts of water. It also destroys the land by removing soil and rocks. Mining some kinds of minerals can poison the water that desert plants and animals need.

ATVs harm deserts

People like to ride all-terrain-vehicles (ATVs) in the deserts of the United States. As they drive over burrows, they kill or hurt animals in them. They also kill desert plants that animals need for food. The tires break up the thin crust on the soil. This allows **erosion** of thin desert soil.

25

People use too much water

The number of people in the world is growing. All these people need food. But growing crops in or near deserts uses lots of water. Much of this water comes from deep wells. Some of this water took thousands of years to collect underground. Using too much water can cause wells to go dry. It can cause desert **oases** to disappear. Lack of water harms all the living things in a desert.

People save water

The Thar Desert receives between 5 and 10 inches (13 and 25 centimeters) of rain each year. But it all falls in about one week during the summer. There is so much rain, the ground cannot soak it up. So farmers build earth dams to trap the water. Then some of it is used to **irrigate** crops. The rest soaks into the ground.

Farmers in the Thar Desert of India and Pakistan use irrigation ditches for their crops.

People keep deserts from spreading

Many countries are trying to reduce **desertification.** Trees and other plants are being planted to hold soil in place. Better ways of farming crops and grazing animals also protect land from becoming a desert.

Sprinklers that spin, like these in Saudia Arabia, can spray large circular fields in deserts.

People reclaim deserts

Desert land can be **reclaimed.** Farmers in the Atacama Desert grow grapefruit trees. Water is pumped from underground for the trees.

Drip **irrigation** is used in the Negev Desert of Israel. Water is pumped through thin plastic pipes. It drips through small holes in the pipes. Each plant gets just enough water. Plastic sheets around the plants keep water from **evaporating.** Crops can grow with little water. Some vegetables are grown in tunnels covered with plastic. This uses even less water.

? **Did you know?**

Some desert **habitats** are protected. Death Valley National Park, in the Mojave Desert, is one of these areas.

Fact File

Desert Areas of the World

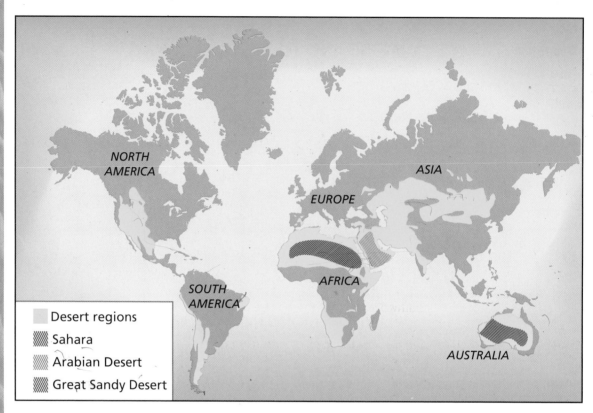

Desert regions
Sahara
Arabian Desert
Great Sandy Desert

Land that is dry and does not get much rain, like deserts, is called arid. Some deserts get more rain than others. The yellow areas on this map show all kinds of desert areas around the world. Parts of the Sahara in Africa are considered extremely arid. The Great Sandy Desert in Australia and the Arabian Desert get a bit more precipitation and are considered arid. The areas around the Great Sandy Desert are semiarid, or partly dry.

Name	Type	Location	Facts
Arabian	hot	Arabian Peninsula	It is covered almost entirely by sand.
Atacama	cool	coasts of Peru and Chile in South America	Large deposits of sodium nitrate are found there; it's used to make gunpowder.
Australian— Great Sandy*	hot	Australia	**Aborigines** have lived in the Australian deserts for over 30,000 years.
Chihuahuan	hot	north central Mexico and southwestern United States	It's the largest desert in North America. Big Bend National Park in Texas is located here.
Gobi and Takla Makan	cold	northern China and southern Mongolia in Asia; western China	The Gobi Desert's name comes from *kobi*, the Mongolian word for waterless place. The Chinese call it *shamo*, which means sandy area.
Iranian	cold	Iran, Afghanistan, and Pakistan in Asia	Parts of this desert have no plant life at all. Hot wind, called Luar, always blows in this desert.
Kalahari	hot	southwestern Africa	The San people have lived in this desert for 20,000 years.
Mojave	hot	southwestern United States	Borax, potash, salt, silver, and tungsten are mined in this desert.
Namib	cool	coasts of southwestern Africa	The world's greatest source of gemstones is on the coast of this desert.
Patagonian	cold	Argentina in South America	People raise sheep in this desert. Fruits, cereals, and potatoes are grown in irrigated places.
Sahara	hot	northern Africa	This desert gets its name from the Arabic word meaning desert.
Sonoran	hot	southwestern United States and parts of Mexico	The Sonoran has more kinds of plants and animals than any other desert in the world.
Thar	hot	India and Pakistan	Small villages of ten to twenty houses are scattered throughout this desert.
Turkestan	cold	parts of the Middle East and southwestern Russia	In ancient times, this desert was crossed by caravans traveling from China to Europe.

* and the Victoria, Simpson, Gibson, and Sturt Deserts

Glossary

aborigine person whose ancestors were the first people to live in a country

adaptation feature that allows a living thing to exist under certain conditions

bacteria living things too small to be seen except with a microscope. Some bacteria are decomposers.

burrow hole dug in the ground by animals

carnivore animal that eats only other animals

consumer living thing that needs plants or other animals for food

decomposer living thing that puts nutrients from dead plants and animals back into the soil, air, and water

desertification spread of deserts into areas that used to have more plants

dune hill of sand built up by the wind

dung animal droppings

erode to move soil by wind, water, or ice

erosion the wearing away of rocks and soil by wind, water, or ice

evaporate to change from a liquid to a gas

extinct no longer lives on Earth

felt thick cloth made by pressing animal hair or wool flat

food chain the path that shows who eats what

food web group of connected food chains

forage wander about in search of food

forager animal or person who wanders about searching for food

fossil traces or remains of ancient living things

graze feed on growing grass and other plants

habitat place where a plant or animal lives

herbivore animal that eats only plants

irrigate supply the land with water

irrigation ways of watering land to grow crops

larvae (singular: larva) young of insects

mineral certain materials that are dug from the earth by mining. Gold, iron, and diamonds are minerals.

mold living thing that uses dead plants and animals for food

mummified dried out dead body

nocturnal active in the night

nomad people who move around from place to place

nutrient material that is needed for growth of a plant or animal

oasis (plural: **oases**) place in the desert where water comes to the surface and plants can grow

omnivore animal that eats plants and animals

photosynthesis process by which green plants trap the sun's energy and use it to change carbon dioxide and water into sugars

predator animal that hunts and eats other animals

prey animal that is hunted and eaten by other animals

producer living thing that can use sunlight to make its own food

reclaim change desert to farmland

scavenge feed on the bodies of dead animals

scavenger animal that eats the bodies of other animals that are already dead

stomata tiny openings in the undersides of leaves

succulent plant that has thick leaves or stems with a waxy coating

yaks kind of wild ox with a shaggy coat

More Books to Read

Fowler, Allan. *Living in a Desert.* Danbury, Conn.: Children's Press, 2000.

Kottke, Jan. *Living in a Desert.* Danbury, Conn.: Children's Press, 2000.

O'Mara, Anna. *Deserts.* Mankato, Minn.: Bridgestone Books, 1999.

Steele, Christy and Frank A. Sloan, ed. *Deserts.* Austin, Tex.: Raintree/Steck Vaughn, 2001.

Stotksy, Sandra. *Discovering Deserts.* Broomall, Penn.: Chelsea House Publishers, 1999.

Index